"The problem with pain is that it can obscure our vision of God, causing us to forget the truths that would sustain our trust through trials. What sufferers need most is to be reminded of the truths we already know in clear, simple, and brief increments. That's why I'm so happy to have *31 Days Toward Trusting God* by one of my favorite authors, Jerry Bridges. Here are a month of meditations for sufferers on the sovereignty, love, and wisdom of God. If you are suffering, know someone who is, or wisely want to prepare for the inevitable suffering that awaits, may this book anchor your confidence in God's goodness and sustaining grace."

—C. J. MAHANEY, senior pastor,
Sovereign Grace Church, Louisville, Kentucky

"Spending a month of quiet times with Jerry Bridges, one of our favorite teachers, has been a real joy. Day by day, he has encouraged and inspired us with clarity and sincerity to trust in God's wisdom, sovereignty, and love. What a privilege it is to learn from this humble man of God who fervently embraces and relies on the Scriptures. His newest book is now at the top of our 'Favorite Gifts to Give' list."

—ANNE ROBINSON AND JOYCE WATSON,
cofounders and codirectors, Mountaintop Conference,
Wheeling, West Virginia

31
DAYS
TOWARD
TRUSTING
GOD

JERRY
BRIDGES

A NavPress resource published in alliance
with Tyndale House Publishers, Inc.

NAVPRESS ●

NavPress is the publishing ministry of The Navigators, an international Christian organization and leader in personal spiritual development. NavPress is committed to helping people grow spiritually and enjoy lives of meaning and hope through personal and group resources that are biblically rooted, culturally relevant, and highly practical.

For more information, visit www.NavPress.com.

31 Days Toward Trusting God

Copyright © 2013 by Jerry Bridges. All rights reserved.

A NavPress resource published in alliance with Tyndale House Publishers, Inc.

NAVPRESS and the NAVPRESS logo are registered trademarks of NavPress, The Navigators, Colorado Springs, CO. *TYNDALE* is a registered trademark of Tyndale House Publishers, Inc. Absence of ® in connection with marks of NavPress or other parties does not indicate an absence of registration of those marks.

Cover design by Arvid Wallen

Adapted from *Trusting God* © 1988, 2008 by Jerry Bridges

Italics in Scripture quotations are the author's emphasis.

Unless otherwise indicated, all Scripture quotations are taken from *The Holy Bible*, English Standard Version® (ESV®), copyright © 2001 by Crossway, a publishing ministry of Good News Publishers. Used by permission. All rights reserved. Scripture quotations marked NIV are taken from the Holy Bible, *New International Version*,® *NIV*.® Copyright © 1973, 1978, 1984, 2011 by Biblica, Inc.® Used by permission. All rights reserved worldwide.

Some of the anecdotal illustrations in this book are true to life and are included with the permission of the persons involved. All other illustrations are composites of real situations, and any resemblance to people living or dead is coincidental.

Library of Congress Cataloging-in-Publication Data

Bridges, Jerry.
  31 days toward trusting God : a daily devotional / Jerry Bridges.
     pages cm
  Includes bibliographical references.
  ISBN 978-1-61291-497-8
  1. Providence and government of God—Christianity. 2. Trust in God. 3. Devotional literature. I. Title. II. Title: Thirty-one days toward trusting God.
  BT96.3.B75 2013
  242'.2—dc23
                                        2013016537

Printed in the United States of America

21 20 19 18 17 16 15
8   7   6   5   4   3   2

CONTENTS

PREFACE

This daily devotional is based on my book *Trusting God Even When Life Hurts*, which was published in the summer of 1988. My wife, Eleanor, died a few months later in November of that year. I actually submitted the finished manuscript to NavPress in December 1987, the same month we learned that Eleanor's cancer had returned in a more virulent form.

So I had eleven months, as I watched Eleanor slowly die, to live out the biblical truths of trusting God that I had just written about. It has now been twenty-five years since *Trusting God Even When Life Hurts* was published. Eleanor's death was only the first of many difficult and sometimes painful experiences I have encountered in those years, and I can testify that the biblical truths I wrote about in 1987 are indeed true. We can trust God even when life hurts.

It is my prayer that these thirty-one daily devotions will serve to remind previous readers of the book about those important truths and that they will introduce new readers to the truth that they can trust God in times of difficulty and pain.

CAN I TRUST GOD?

*Take care, brothers, lest there be in any of you
an evil, unbelieving heart, leading you to
fall away from the living God.*
HEBREWS 3:12

For most of us, life is filled with frustrations, anxieties, and disappointments that tempt us to fret, fume, and worry. One author has aptly captured the flavor of this in a devotional book for high schoolers titled *If God Loves Me, Why Can't I Get My Locker Open?* We may smile a little at that, but the fact is, this is the plane of adversity on which many of us live each day. And it's in the crucible of even this minor level of adversity that we're tempted to wonder, *Can I trust God?*

Even when life seems to be going our way and our daily path seems pleasant and smooth, we don't know what the future holds, just as Solomon has said: "You do not know what a day may bring" (Proverbs 27:1). Someone has described life as like having a thick curtain hung across one's path, receding before us as we advance, but only step-by-step. None of us can tell what's beyond that curtain; none of us can tell what events a single day or hour might bring into our lives. Sometimes the retreating curtain reveals events much as we had expected; often it reveals things unexpected and undesired, filling us with anxiety, frustration, heartache, and grief.

God's people are not immune from such pain. In fact, it often seems as if theirs is more severe, more frequent, more unexplainable, and more deeply felt than the pain of the unbeliever. The problem of pain is as old as history and just as universal. Even creation itself, Paul tells us, has been subjected to frustration and groans as in the pains of childbirth (see Romans 8:20-22).

So the question naturally arises, "Where is God in all of this?" Can you really trust God when adversity strikes and fills your life with pain? Does He indeed come to the rescue of those who seek Him? Does He truly deliver those who call upon Him in the day of trouble, as Psalm 50:15 promises? Does the Lord's unfailing love in fact surround the person who trusts in Him, as Psalm 32:10 affirms?

Psalm 50:15 and call on me in the day of trouble I will deliver you and you will honor me.

Many are the woes of the wicked but the Lord's unfailing love surrounds the one who trusts in him.

31 DAYS TOWARD TRUSTING GOD

I sympathize with those who find it particularly difficult to trust God in times of adversity. I've been there myself often enough to know something of the distress, despair, and darkness that fill our souls when we wonder if God truly cares about our plight. I've spent a good portion of my adult life encouraging people to pursue holiness, to obey God, yet I acknowledge it often seems more difficult to trust God than to obey Him.

God's moral will as seen in the Bible is rational and reasonable, but the circumstances in which we must trust God often appear irrational and inexplicable. God's law is readily recognized as being good for us, but the circumstances of our lives frequently appear harmful and grim, perhaps even calamitous and tragic. Obeying God is worked out within well-defined boundaries of God's revealed will, while trusting God must be worked out in an arena with no boundaries, where we're always coping with the unknown.

Yet it's just as important to trust God as to obey Him. When we disobey God, we defy His authority and despise His holiness. And when we fail to trust Him, we doubt His sovereignty and question His goodness. In both cases, we cast aspersions upon His majesty and His character. God views both with equal seriousness. When the people of Israel were hungry, "they spoke against God, saying, 'Can God spread a table in the wilderness? . . . Can he also give bread or provide meat for his people?'" (Psalm 78:19-20). The next two verses tell us, "When the LORD heard, he was full of wrath . . . because *they did not believe in God and did not trust his saving power.*"

In order to trust God, we must always view our adverse circumstances through the eyes of faith, not of sense.

- What is God trying to teach us through the adversity that he brings into our lives, ...

- Have faith that he does this to bring us closer to him ??

SUSTAINING ALL THINGS

He is before all things, and in him all things hold together.

COLOSSIANS 1:17

The Bible teaches that God not only created the universe but also upholds and sustains it day by day, hour by hour. Scripture says that Christ, the Son of God, "upholds the universe by the word of his power" (Hebrews 1:3). As theologian A. H. Strong said, "Christ is the originator and upholder of the universe. . . . In him it consists, or holds together, from hour to hour. The steady will of Christ constitutes the law of the universe and makes it a cosmos instead of a chaos, just as his will brought it into being in the beginning."[1]

All things are indebted for their existence to the continuous sustaining action of God exercised through His Son. Nothing exists of its own inherent power of being. Nothing in all creation stands or acts independently of the Lord's will. The so-called laws of nature are nothing more than the physical expression of the steady will of Christ. The law of gravity operates with unceasing certainty because Christ continuously wills it to operate. The chair I am sitting on while I write these words holds together because the atoms and molecules in the wood are held in place by His active will.

Is this thinking beyond my faith?

The stars continue in their courses because He keeps them there. It is God "who brings out their host by number, calling them all by name, by the greatness of his might, and because he is strong in power not one is missing" (Isaiah 40:26).

God's sustaining action in Christ goes beyond the inanimate creation. The Bible says that He gives life to everything: "He prepares rain for the earth; he makes grass grow on the hills. He gives to the beasts their food, and to the young ravens that cry" (Psalm 147:8-9; see also Nehemiah 9:6).

God did not simply create and then walk away. He constantly sustains that which He created.

Further, the Bible teaches that God sustains not only the universe around us but also you and me: "He himself gives to

God anointed out our times & places so that we would seek him + perhaps reach out for him, find him – as he is not far from us.

all mankind life and breath and everything . . . for 'In him we live and move and have our being'" (Acts 17:25,28). He supplies our daily food (see 2 Corinthians 9:10). Our times are in His hand (see Psalm 31:15).

Every breath we breathe is a gift from God; every bite of food we eat is given to us from His hand; every day we live is determined by Him. He has not left us to our own devices or the whims of nature or the malevolent acts of other people. No! He constantly sustains, provides for, and cares for us every moment of every day. Did your car break down when you could least afford the repairs? Did you miss an important meeting because the plane you were to fly in developed mechanical problems? The God who controls the stars in their courses also controls nuts and bolts and everything on your car and on that plane you were to fly in.

When I was an infant, I had a bad case of measles. The virus apparently settled in my eyes and in my right ear, leaving me with lifelong impaired vision and hearing. Was God in control of that virus, or was I simply a victim of a chance childhood disease? God's moment-by-moment sustaining of His universe and everything in it leaves me no choice but to accept that the virus was indeed under His controlling hand. God was not looking the other way when that virus settled in the nerve endings of my ear and the muscles of my eyes. If we are to trust God, we must learn to see that He is continuously at work in every aspect and every moment of our lives.

All this is what we call divine providence—God's sustaining and governing His universe, bringing all things and events to their appointed end. Even our suffering has meaning and purpose in God's eternal plan, for He brings or allows into our lives only that which is for His glory and our good.

CONFIDENCE IN GOD'S SOVEREIGNTY

*Our God is in the heavens; he
does all that he pleases.*
PSALM 115:3

God does whatever pleases Him. This is the essence of God's
sovereignty: His absolute independence to do as He pleases
and His absolute control over the actions of all His creatures.
No creature, person, or empire can either thwart His will or
act outside the bounds of it.

Even the mistakes and failures of other people are under
God's control. Did another driver go through a red light, strike
your car, and send you to the hospital with multiple fractures?

Did a physician fail to detect your cancer in its early stages, when it was treatable? Did you end up with an incompetent instructor in an important course in college or an inept supervisor who blocked your career? All these circumstances are under God's controlling hand, as He works them out for our good.

Not even the willfully malicious acts of others can sidetrack God's purpose for us: "No wisdom, no understanding, no counsel can avail against the LORD" (Proverbs 21:30). The Roman governor Felix unjustly left Paul in prison for two years for his own political reasons (see Acts 24:27); Joseph was left in prison for two years because Pharaoh's cupbearer forgot him (see Genesis 40:14,23; 41:1). These two godly men were left to languish behind bars — one because of deliberate injustice, the other because of inexcusable forgetfulness. Yet both predicaments were sovereignly directed by an infinitely wise and loving God.

Nothing is so small or trivial as to escape God's control; nothing is so great as to be beyond His power to govern it. The insignificant sparrow cannot fall to the ground without His will (see Matthew 10:29); the mighty Roman Empire cannot crucify Jesus unless that power is given by God (see John 19:10-11). And what is true for the sparrow and for Jesus is true for you and me. No detail of life is too insignificant for our heavenly Father's attention; no circumstance is so big that He cannot handle it.

Confidence in God's total sovereignty is crucial to our trusting Him. If there's a single event in all the universe that could occur outside His control, then we cannot trust Him. However infinite His love, if His power is limited and His purpose preventable, we cannot trust Him.

You may entrust to me your most valuable possessions; I may aim sincerely and lovingly to honor that trust. But if I'm unable to guard your valuables, you cannot truly entrust them to me. Paul, however, said we can entrust our most valuable possessions to the Lord: "I know whom I have believed, and am convinced that he is able to guard what I have entrusted to him until that day" (2 Timothy 1:12, NIV).

"But," someone says, "Paul is speaking there of eternal life. It's our problems in *this* life that make me wonder about God's sovereignty." It should be evident, however, that God's sovereignty doesn't begin at death. His sovereign direction in our lives even precedes our births. God rules as surely on earth as He does in heaven. For reasons known only to Him, He permits people to act contrary to and in defiance of His heart and character, but He never permits them to act contrary to His sovereign will.

Our plans turn out well only when they are consistent with God's purpose, and no plan can succeed against Him (see Proverbs 16:9; 19:21; 21:30). No one can straighten what He makes crooked or make crooked what He has made straight (see Ecclesiastes 7:13). No one can say, "I'll do this or that," and have it happen if it is not part of God's sovereign will (see James 4:15).

What an encouragement and stimulus to trusting God this aspect of God's sovereignty should be to us! God is in control, although within His control, He allows us to experience pain. That pain is very real; we hurt, we suffer. But in the midst of our suffering, we must believe what author Margaret Clarkson has written: "God is the Lord of human history and of the personal history of every member of His redeemed family."[2]

HIS WISE AND LOVING PLAN FOR ME

*In him we have obtained an inheritance,
having been predestined according to
the purpose of him who works all things
according to the counsel of his will.*
EPHESIANS 1:11

The bare thought that God does only as He pleases would terrify us if that were all we knew about God. But He is not only sovereign; He is also perfect in love and infinite in wisdom. God always exercises His sovereignty for His glory and the good of His people.

But how is this any more than merely an abstract

statement about God to be debated by the theologians, a statement that has little relevance to our day-to-day lives?

The answer is that God does have a purpose and a plan for you, and He has the power to carry out that plan. It's one thing to know that no person or circumstance can touch us outside of God's sovereign control; it's still another to realize that no person or circumstance can frustrate God's purpose for our lives.

God's overarching purpose for all believers is to conform us to the likeness of Jesus: "Those whom he foreknew he also predestined to be conformed to the image of his Son" (Romans 8:29). He also has a specific purpose for each of us that is His unique, tailor-made plan for our individual life: "We are his workmanship, created in Christ Jesus for good works, which God prepared beforehand, that we should walk in them" (Ephesians 2:10).

God *will* fulfill that personal plan for us. As David said in Psalm 138:8, "The LORD will fulfill his purpose for me." Because we know God is directing our lives to an ultimate end and because we know He is sovereignly able to orchestrate the events of our lives toward that end, we can trust Him. We can commit to Him not only the ultimate outcome of our lives but also all the intermediate events and circumstances that will bring us to that outcome.

Still, it's difficult for us to fully appreciate the reality of

Faith in what is not Seen

God's sovereignly doing as He pleases in our lives because we don't see Him doing anything. Instead, we see ourselves or other people acting and events occurring, and we evaluate those actions and events according to our own preferences and plans. We see ourselves influencing or perhaps even controlling or being controlled by the actions of other people, but we don't see God at work.

But over all the actions and events of our lives, God is in control, doing as He pleases—not apart from those events or in spite of them but *through* them. Joseph's brothers sold him into slavery—a malicious act in and of itself—but in due time, Joseph recognized that through his brothers' actions, God was acting. Joseph could say to them, "It was not you who sent me here, but God" (Genesis 45:8). Joseph recognized the hand of God in his life sovereignly directing all the events to bring about His plan for him.

You and I may never have the privilege in this life of seeing an obvious outcome of God's plan for us, as Joseph did. But God's plan for us is no less firm and its outcome no less certain than was God's plan for Joseph. God did not give us the story of Joseph's life just to inform us but also to encourage us: "Whatever was written in former days was written for our instruction, that through endurance and *through the encouragement of the Scriptures* we might have hope" (Romans 15:4).

What God did for Joseph, He will do for us. But to derive the comfort and encouragement from this truth God has provided, we must learn to trust Him. We must learn to walk, as Paul said, "by faith, not by sight" (2 Corinthians 5:7).

And so "we look not to the things that are seen but to the things that are unseen. For the things that are seen are transient, but the things that are unseen are eternal" (4:18).

A WAY TO HONOR
GOD

*I know the plans I have for you, declares
the Lord, plans for welfare and not for evil,
to give you a future and a hope.*

JEREMIAH 29:11

Jeremiah 29:11 is a passage that has been meaningful to me for several years. Although its words were directed to the nation of Judah in its captivity, they express a principle that's affirmed elsewhere throughout the Bible: God has a plan for you. And because no one can thwart that plan, you can have hope and courage. You too can trust God.

From our limited vantage point, our lives are marked by

an endless series of contingencies. Instead of acting as we planned, we frequently find ourselves *reacting* to an unexpected turn of events. We make plans but are often forced to change them.

Even those whose lives are free from major pain still experience the frequently frustrating or anxiety-producing events of daily life, which momentarily grab our attention and rob us of our peace of mind. A long-planned vacation has to be cancelled because of illness, the washing machine breaks down the day company arrives, your class notes are lost or stolen the day before a major exam, you tear your favorite dress on the way to church, and on and on. Instances of this magnitude are numerous. Life is full of them.

But there are no contingencies with God. Our unexpected, forced change of plans is a part of His plan. God is never surprised, never caught off guard, never frustrated by unexpected developments. God does as He pleases, and that which pleases Him is always for His glory and our good.

Our lives are also cluttered with a lot of "if onlys": "If only I had done this," or "If only that had not happened." But again, God has no "if onlys." God never makes a mistake; God has no regrets. "This God—his way is perfect" (Psalm 18:30). We can trust God. He is trustworthy.

And so we're told, "Trust in him at all times, O people; pour out your heart before him; God is a refuge for us" (62:8).

Such encouragement is needed because so often our faith falters in various situations while we await the outcome. And frequently our situations don't really have a happy ending. Is God sovereign then also? This is the crucial question.

It's difficult to believe that God is in control when we're in the midst of heartache or grief. I've struggled with this many times myself. So often I've had to *decide* whether I would trust Him when my heart ached. I continually realize anew that we must learn to trust God one circumstance at a time.

It's not a matter of my feelings but of my will. I never feel like trusting God when adversity strikes, but I can choose to do so anyway. That act of the will must be based on belief, and belief must be based on the truth that God is sovereign. He carries out His own good purposes without ever being thwarted, and nothing is outside His sovereign will. We must cling to this in the face of adversity and tragedy if we're to glorify God by trusting Him.

I'll say this as gently and compassionately as I know how: Our first priority in adversity is to honor and glorify God by trusting Him. Gaining relief from our feelings of heartache or disappointment or frustration is a natural desire (see 2 Corinthians 12:9), and God has promised to give us grace sufficient for our trials and peace for our anxieties (see Philippians 4:6-7). But just as God's will is to take precedence over our will ("Not as I will, but as you will" [Matthew 26:39]), so God's honor is to take precedence over our feelings.

We honor God by choosing to trust Him when we don't understand what He is doing or why He has allowed some adverse circumstance to occur. As we seek God's glory, we may be sure He has purposed our good and won't be frustrated in fulfilling that purpose.

GOD'S SOVEREIGNTY OVER OTHER PEOPLE

If God is for us, who can be against us?
Romans 8:31

All of us at times find ourselves and our futures seemingly in the hands of other people. Their decisions or actions determine whether we get a good grade or a poor one, whether we're promoted or fired, whether our career blossoms or folds. Sometimes those decisions or actions are benevolent and good; sometimes they're wicked or careless. Either way, they affect us, often in a significant way.

How are we to respond when we find ourselves desperately needing a favorable decision or action on another person's part? Can we trust God that He'll work in the heart of that individual to bring about His plan for us? Or consider the instance when someone is out to ruin our reputation or jeopardize our career. Can we trust God to intervene in that person's heart so he doesn't carry out his evil intent?

According to the Bible, the answer is yes. God does sovereignly intervene in people's hearts so that their decisions and actions accomplish His purpose for our lives. Perhaps the clearest statement of this is in Proverbs 21:1: "The king's heart is a stream of water in the hand of the LORD; he turns it wherever he will." Charles Bridges comments that here the "general truth" of God's sovereignty over the hearts of all people "is taught by the strongest illustration — his uncontrollable sway upon the most absolute of all wills — the king's heart."[3]

In our day of limited monarchies, it may be difficult to appreciate fully the force of what Charles Bridges is saying. But in Solomon's time, the king was an absolute monarch. There was no separate legislative body to make laws he wouldn't like or a Supreme Court to restrain him. The king's word was law. His authority over his realm was unconditional and unrestrained. Yet God controls that king's heart. The stubborn will of the most powerful monarch on earth is directed by God as easily as the farmer directs the flow of water in his irrigation canals. And if God controls the king's heart, surely He controls everyone else's. All must move before His sovereign influence.

That is the Bible's consistent teaching. Yet it also seems equally clear from Scripture that God does this without violating or coercing their wills but rather works in His mysterious way through their own free and voluntary choices to accomplish His purposes.

God is never at a loss because He cannot find someone to cooperate with Him in carrying out His plans. He so moves in the hearts of people — either Christians or non-Christians, it makes no difference — that they willingly, of their own free, will carry out His plans. Do you need the good favor of a certain professor in order to get a good recommendation for a job? If that job is God's plan for you, God is able to and will move in the heart of that professor to give you a good recommendation.

Are you dependent upon your boss (or your commanding officer or some other person) for advancement in your career? God will move in the heart of that person one way or the other, depending on His plan for you (see Psalm 75:6-7).

Your promotion, or lack of it, is in the hand of God. Your superiors are simply His agents to carry out His will. They are not conscious of doing His will and never intended to do it (unless, of course, they are Christians prayerfully seeking to follow the will of God), but that does not alter the result in your life.

You can trust God in all the areas of your life where you

are dependent upon the favor or frown of another person. God will move in that person's heart to carry out His will for you. Our destinies are in His hands, not the hands of bosses, commanding officers, professors, coaches, or any others. No one can influence your future apart from the sovereign will of God. You can entrust your future to God.

TRUSTING GOD IN PHYSICAL AFFLICTION

Though he cause grief, he will have
compassion according to the
abundance of his steadfast love;
for he does not afflict from his heart
or grieve the children of men.
LAMENTATIONS 3:32-33

When babies are born with major birth defects, or cancer strikes, or a loved one experiences continuous pain for years without relief, we often struggle to trust God. Even if we're normally healthy and strong, we often experience sicknesses at the most inopportune times. Is God truly sovereign over the diseases and physical infirmities that so frequently afflict us?

When God called Moses to lead the Israelites out of Egypt, Moses protested his inadequacy, including the fact that he was slow of speech. God's reply to Moses is instructive: "Who has made man's mouth? Who makes him mute, or deaf, or seeing, or blind? Is it not I, the LORD?" (Exodus 4:11). Here God specifically ascribes to His own work the physical afflictions of deafness, muteness, and blindness. These physical afflictions are not merely the products of defective genes or birth accidents; behind them all is the sovereign purpose of God. When asked about a man blind from birth, Jesus replied, "This happened so that the works of God might be displayed in him" (John 9:3, NIV).

This God of deafness, muteness, and blindness is also the God of cancer, arthritis, Down syndrome, and all other such afflictions that strike us. None of them "just happen"; they're all within the sovereign will of God.

Such a statement immediately brings us into the problem of pain and suffering. Why does a sovereign God who loves us allow such pain and heartache?

We know that the ultimate cause of all pain and suffering must be traced back to the sin of Adam and its effect on all creation (see Romans 8:20) as part of God's determined response to man's sin. The sovereign God who subjected creation to frustration still rules over that creation, pain and all. The laws of genetics and disease are as much under His sway as are the laws of meteorology. To trust Him, we have to be convinced that He's in sovereign control over every physical area of our lives. If He's not—if illness and afflictions "just happen"—then of course there's no basis for trusting God. But if He is sovereign in these areas, we can trust Him, even without understanding all the theological issues involved in the problem of pain.

We can also find assurance in the fact that God does not *willingly* bring affliction or grief our way (see Lamentations 3:32-33). He has no delight in our experience of pain or heartache. He always has a purpose for the grief He allows into our lives. Most often we don't know what that purpose is, but it's enough to know that His infinite wisdom and perfect love have determined that this particular sorrow is best for us. God never wastes pain; He always uses it to accomplish His purpose. And His purpose is for His glory and our good. Therefore, we can trust Him when our hearts are aching or our bodies are racked with pain.

Trusting God in the midst of pain and heartache means that we actually accept these things from Him. This is different from mere resignation. We can resign ourselves to a difficult situation simply because we see no other alternative. People do that all the time. Or we can submit to God's sovereignty in our circumstances with a certain amount of reluctance. But to truly accept pain and heartache includes our willingness. An attitude of acceptance says, "I trust God, knowing He loves me and gives only what's best for me."

Acceptance doesn't mean we don't pray for healing or for relief from physical problems. We should indeed pray for such things, but we should pray in a trusting way. We should realize that though God can do all things—for infinitely wise and loving reasons—He may not do what we ask Him to do. So we keep praying, as long as we can do so trustingly, with an attitude of acceptance of His will.

GOD'S SOVEREIGNTY AND MY RESPONSIBILITY

Trust in the Lord, and do good.

Psalm 37:3

As we recognize what the Scriptures teach about God's sovereignty, we need to be cautious not to misuse or abuse this doctrine.

God's sovereignty does not negate our responsibility to pray but rather makes it possible to pray with confidence. Prayer assumes God's sovereignty. Otherwise, we have no assurance that He's able to answer those prayers; they would become nothing more than wishes. God's sovereignty (along with His wisdom and love) remains the foundation of our trust in Him, while prayer represents the expression of that trust.

Nor does God's sovereignty set aside our responsibility to act prudently—to use all legitimate means at our disposal to avoid harming ourselves or others and to bring about what is good and right. God usually works through means, and He intends that we use them as He makes them available. Of course, unless God prospers those means, all our plans, efforts, and prudence are of no avail.

In Psalm 127:1, we find a memorable illustration of this truth:

> Unless the LORD builds the house,
>   those who build it labor in vain.
> Unless the LORD watches over the city,
>   the watchman stays awake in vain.

In a sense, the verse sums up all our responsibilities in life. Whether in the physical, the mental, or the spiritual realm, we should always be building and watching, always recognizing that none of these efforts will prosper unless God intervenes.

At the same time, we remain responsible. The Bible never allows us to use our utter dependence on God as an excuse for indolence. "Sluggards do not plow in season; so at harvest time they look but find nothing" (Proverbs 20:4, NIV). We're absolutely dependent upon God yet simultaneously responsible to diligently use whatever means are appropriate for the occasion.

So does failure on our part to act prudently frustrate the sovereign plan of God?

The Scriptures never indicate that God is frustrated to any degree by our failure to act as wisely as we should. In His own infinite wisdom, God's sovereign plan includes our failures and even our sins.

When Mordecai asked Queen Esther to intercede with King Xerxes on behalf of the Jews, she demurred, explaining that she could enter the king's presence unbidden only on the threat of death (see Esther 4:10-11). However, Mordecai sent word back to her: "If you keep silent at this time, relief and deliverance will rise for the Jews from another place, but you and your father's house will perish. And who knows whether you have not come to the kingdom for such a time as this?" (verse 14). The key phrase here is this: Relief and deliverance will rise for the Jews from another place.

The options available to God to bring about deliverance for the Jews were as infinite as His wisdom and power. He literally did not need Esther's cooperation. But in this instance, He chose to use her. Mordecai's words assume that God uses people and means to accomplish His sovereign purpose. As subsequent events proved, God had indeed raised up Esther to accomplish His purpose. But He could just as easily have raised up someone else or used an altogether different means.

God usually works through ordinary events (as opposed to miracles) and the voluntary actions of people. But He always provides the means necessary and guides them by His unseen hand. He is sovereign, and He cannot be frustrated by our failure to act or by any of our actions that in themselves are sinful. We must always remember, however, that God still holds us accountable for the very sins He uses to accomplish His purpose.

There's no conflict in the Bible between His sovereignty and our responsibility. Both are taught with equal force and with no attempt to "reconcile" them. Let us hold equally to both, doing our duty as revealed in Scripture and trusting God to sovereignly work out His purpose in and through us.

TRUSTING GOD'S WISDOM

As the heavens are higher than the earth,
so are my ways higher than your ways
and my thoughts than your thoughts.

ISAIAH 55:9

God never has to agonize over a decision or even deliberate within Himself or consult others. His wisdom is intuitive, infinite, and infallible: "His understanding has no limit" (Psalm 147:5, NIV).

As we observe events that seem senselessly tragic or experience adversity ourselves, we often fail to see any possible good to us or glory to God that can come from it. But is not the wisdom of God—and thus His glory—more eminently displayed in bringing good out of calamity than out of blessing?

There's no question that God's people live in a hostile world. We have an enemy, the Devil, who "prowls around like a roaring lion, seeking someone to devour" (1 Peter 5:8). He wants to sift us like wheat as he did Peter (see Luke 22:31) or make us curse God as he tried to get Job to do. God doesn't spare us from the ravages of disease, heartache, and disappointment in this sin-cursed world. But He is able to take all these elements—the bad as well as the good—and make full use of every one. His infinite wisdom is thus displayed in bringing good out of evil, beauty out of ashes. It's displayed in turning all the forces of evil that rage against His children into something for their good, though often a far different good than we envision.

God in His infinite wisdom knows exactly what we need to grow more into the likeness of His Son. He not only knows what we need but also when and how best to bring it into our lives. He's the perfect teacher and coach. His discipline is always exactly suited for us. For example, He never "overtrains" us by allowing too much adversity in our lives, the kind of difficulties that raise so many "why" questions for us.

Three of the psalms begin with *why*: "Why, O LORD, do you stand far away? Why do you hide yourself in times of trouble?" (10:1); "My God, my God, why have you forsaken me? Why are you so far from saving me, from the words of my groaning?" (22:1); "O God, why do you cast us off forever? Why does your anger smoke against the sheep of your pasture?" (74:1). But each of those psalms ends on a note of trust in God. These psalmists didn't allow their whys to drag on or to take root and grow into accusations against God. Their whys were really cries of anguish, a natural reaction to pain.

Though we should never be demanding, we may and should ask God to enable us to understand what He's teaching us through a particular experience. But even here, we must trust that He's working in these experiences for our good, even when we recognize no beneficial results. We must learn to trust God when He doesn't tell us why and we don't understand what He's doing.

We'll never fully understand. In Paul's doxology at the end of Romans 11, he exclaims in amazement, "Oh, the depth of the riches and wisdom and knowledge of God! How unsearchable are his judgments and how inscrutable his ways!" (verse 33). God's wisdom is fathomless, His decisions unsearchable, His methods mysterious and untraceable. No one has ever understood His mind, let alone advised Him on the proper course of action. We step over a moral line when we arrogantly demand that God tell us what He is doing in a particular event or circumstance. This is futile and even sinful, for we simply cannot search out the reasons behind His decisions or trace out the ways by which He brings those decisions to pass.

We must come to truly accept that God's ways are simply beyond us. This may seem like an intellectual cop-out, a refusal to deal with life's tough issues. In fact, it's just the opposite. It's a surrender to the truth about God and our circumstances as revealed by God Himself in His inspired Word.

WHEN I QUESTION GOD'S LOVE

*He who did not spare his own Son but gave
him up for us all, how will he not also
with him graciously give us all things?*

ROMANS 8:32

It seems the more we accept God's sovereignty over our lives, the more we're tempted to question His love. We think, *If God can do something about this adversity, why doesn't He?*

There's no doubt the most convincing evidence of God's love in all of Scripture is His giving His Son to die for our sins. It's very important that we grasp the crucial concept that God's love to us is *in Christ.* God's infinite, measureless love is poured out upon us not because of who or what we are but because we are in Christ Jesus, because of what He has done for us in the gospel.

In Romans 8:38-39, Paul declared that *nothing* "will be able to separate us from *the love of God in Christ Jesus our Lord*." God's love flows to us entirely through, or in, Jesus Christ. Paul frequently uses the term *in Christ* to refer to our spiritually organic union with Jesus Christ. Jesus speaks of this same union in His metaphor of the vine and its branches in John 15. Just as the branches are organically related to the vine in a life-giving union, so believers, in a spiritual sense, are organically united to Christ.

Just as God's love to His Son cannot change, so His love to us cannot change because we're in union with the One He loves. God's love to us can no more waver than His love to His Son can waver.

We're constantly tempted to look within ourselves to seek to find some reason God should love us. Such searching is, of course, usually discouraging; we instead find so many reasons God should *not* love us. But the Bible is clear that God doesn't look within us for a reason to love us. Rather, as He looks at us, He sees us united to His beloved Son, clothed in His righteousness. He loves us not because we are lovely in ourselves but because we are in Christ.

Here then is another weapon of truth we should store up

in our hearts to use against our doubts and the temptation to question God's love for us: God's love to us cannot fail any more than His love to Christ can fail.

When we begin questioning the love of God, we need to remember who we are. We have absolutely no claim on His love. We don't deserve one bit of God's goodness to us. I once heard a speaker say, "Anything this side of hell is pure grace." Nothing cuts quicker the nerve of a petulant "Why me?" attitude than a realization of who we are in God's eyes, apart from Christ.

God loved us when we were totally unworthy, when there was nothing whatsoever within us that would call forth His love. Anytime we're tempted to doubt God's love for us, we should go back to the cross and reason in this fashion: *If God loved me enough to give His Son to die for me when I was His enemy, surely He loves me enough to care for me now that I am His child. Having loved me to the ultimate extent at the cross, He cannot possibly fail to love me in my times of adversity. Having given such a priceless gift as His Son, surely He will also give all else that is consistent with His glory and my good.*

The apostle John said, "God is love" (1 John 4:8). This succinct statement, along with its parallel one, "God is light" (1:5; that is, God is holy), sums up the essential character of God, as revealed to us in Christ and in Scripture. Just as it is impossible in the very nature of God for Him to be anything but perfectly holy, so it is impossible for Him to be anything but perfectly good, "for as high as the heavens are above the earth, so great is his steadfast love toward those who fear him" (Psalm 103:11).

A LOVE NEVER FAILING

Steadfast love surrounds the
one who trusts in the LORD.
PSALM 32:10

God's love cannot fail. It is steadfast, constant, and fixed. In all the adversities we go through, God's love is unfailing. As He says to us in Isaiah 54:10,

"The mountains may depart
   and the hills be removed,
but my steadfast love shall not depart from you,

and my covenant of peace shall not be
removed,"
says the LORD, who has compassion on you.

Because His love cannot fail, He will allow into our lives
only the pain and heartache that is for our ultimate good.
Even the grief that He Himself brings into our lives is tempered
with His compassion. "Though he cause grief, he will have
compassion according to the abundance of his steadfast love"
(Lamentations 3:32). Even the fires of affliction will be
tempered by His compassion, which arises out of His unfailing
love.

God brought grief into Paul's life for his good, but he also
showed compassion, saying to him, "My grace is sufficient for
you" (2 Corinthians 12:9). He provided Paul with the divine
resources to meet the trials.

I think of a physician whose son was born with an incurable birth defect, leaving him crippled for life. I asked the
father how he felt when he, who had dedicated his life to
treating the illnesses of other people, was confronted with an
incurable condition in his own son. He told me his biggest
problem was his tendency to capsule the next twenty years of
his son's life into that initial moment when he learned of his
son's condition. Viewed that way, the adversity was over-
whelming. God does not give twenty years of grace today.

Rather, He gives it day by day. As the song says, "Day by day, and with each passing moment, strength I find to meet my trials here."[4]

God's love means especially that He is *with us* in our troubles. He does not merely send grace from heaven to meet our trials. He Himself comes to help us. "Fear not," He says to us, "I am the one who helps you" (Isaiah 41:14). He promises,

> When you pass through the waters, *I will be with you;*
>   and through the rivers, they shall not overwhelm you;
> when you walk through fire you shall not be burned,
>   and the flame shall not consume you. (43:2)

He will not spare us from the waters of sorrow and the fires of adversity, but He will go through them with us, regardless of their nature or cause.

It's often in the very midst of our adversities that we experience the most delightful manifestations of His love, "for as we share abundantly in Christ's sufferings, so through Christ we share abundantly in comfort too" (2 Corinthians 1:5).

Christ identifies with us in our distresses. When He confronted Saul on the road to Damascus, He said, "Saul, Saul, why are you persecuting me?" And in answer to Saul's question "Who are you, Lord?" He replied, "I am Jesus, whom you are persecuting" (Acts 9:4-5). Because His people were in union with Him, to persecute them was to persecute Him. This truth is no different today. You're in union with Christ just as surely as the disciples were in the time of the book of Acts. And because of this union, Christ shares your adversities.

In whatever way we view our adversities, we find that God's grace is sufficient, His love adequate.

We will almost always struggle with doubts about God's love during our times of adversity. If we never had to struggle, our faith would not grow. But we must engage in the struggle with our doubts; we must not let them overwhelm us. During seemingly intolerable times, we may feel like David, who said at a time of great distress, "How long, O LORD? Will you forget me forever? How long will you hide your face from me?" (Psalm 13:1).

You and I, like David, must wrestle with our thoughts. With God's help, we too can come to the place, even in the midst of our adversities, where we will be able to say, "I trust in Your unfailing love."

GOD MADE ME
WHO I AM

*You formed my inward parts; you knitted
me together in my mother's womb.*
PSALM 139:13

I can still remember trying to play baseball as a youngster in elementary school. I could neither bat nor catch well because I couldn't tell where the ball was or judge how fast it was coming toward me. Only years later did I realize I had monocular vision, being able to focus only one eye at a time. (Depth perception is based on binocular vision, in which both eyes focus together to produce a three-dimensional effect.) Unable to play baseball with the other boys, I felt shame and rejection because I was not like they were.

I've had this vision problem all my life. I could never play tennis and wouldn't dare step into a handball or racquetball court.

Of course, many people have physical or mental impairments much worse than mine. But whether major or minor, these disabilities often cause childhood heartache and then, later on, difficulty with self-acceptance as an adult. When such people become Christians, they might begin to struggle with God over their disabilities and limitations. Life seems to bring continuing adversity simply from who they are.

Their greatest need in trusting God may be to "trust God for who I am." For those with this need, Psalm 139:13-16 has important and helpful things to say.

This passage teaches us that we are who we are because God Himself created us the way we are, not because of any impersonal biological process. Notice in verse 13 that David pictures God as a master weaver at work in our mother's womb, creating us as directly as He created Adam out of the dust of the earth.

Obviously, David was aware of the biological process God used to bring him into this world. He does not deny that; rather, he teaches us that God so superintends the biological process that He is directly involved in fashioning each of us into the person He wants us to be.

In this verse, David also acknowledges, "You formed my inward parts." The Hebrew term here for "inward parts" was used to express the seat of longings and desires and "the innermost center of emotions and of moral sensitivity."[5] David is essentially saying, "You created not only my physical body but also my personality." David was the person he was because God created him that way, physically, mentally, and emotionally.

God was just as personally and directly involved in creating you and me as He was with David. Rev. James Hufstetler instructs us well:

> You are the result of the attentive, careful, thoughtful, intimate, detailed, creative work of God. Your personality, your sex, your height, your features are what they are because God made them *precisely* that way. He made you the way he did because that is the way he wants you to be. . . . If God had wanted you to be basically and creatively different he would have made you differently. Your genes and chromosomes and creaturely distinctives—even the shape of your nose and ears—are what they are by God's design.[6]

Psalm 139:13 isn't the only Bible passage that speaks of God's direct creation of each of us. Job said to God, "Your hands fashioned and made me. . . . Remember that you have made me like clay. . . . You clothed me with skin and flesh, and knit me together with bones and sinews" (Job 10:8-9,11). Likewise, the author of Psalm 119 wrote, "Your hands have made and fashioned me" (verse 73). And God said to Jeremiah, "Before I formed you in the womb I knew you" (Jeremiah 1:5).

The application of the recurring truth in these passages should be clear: If I have difficulty accepting myself the way God made me, then I have a controversy with God.

Obviously, you and I need to change insofar as our sinful nature distorts that which God has made. Therefore, I do not say that we need to accept ourselves merely "as we are" but rather that we must accept ourselves *as God made us* in our basic physical, mental, and emotional makeup.

TRUSTING GOD FOR WHO I AM

*Blessed be the L*ORD *. . . who alone*
does wondrous things.
PSALM 72:18

Instead of fretting over the way God made him, David said, "I praise you because I am fearfully and wonderfully made" (Psalm 139:14, NIV). We might say, "That's well enough for David; he was handsome, athletic, skilled in war, and a gifted musician. But look at me. I'm very ordinary." In fact, some people feel they don't even measure up to ordinary.

I understand those who feel that way. In addition to having hearing and vision disabilities, I've never been excited about my physical appearance. But God didn't give His own Son handsome features in His human body: "He had no beauty or majesty to attract us to him, nothing in his appearance that we should desire him" (Isaiah 53:2, NIV). Jesus, at best, was apparently nondescript in His physical appearance. This never bothered Him nor interfered with His carrying out His Father's will.

David praised God not because he was handsome but because God made him. Dwell on that thought. The eternal God, infinite in His wisdom and perfect in His love, personally made you and me. He gave you your body, your mental abilities, and your basic personality because that's the way He wanted you to be, and He loves you and wants to glorify Himself through you.

This is our foundation for self-acceptance. God sovereignly and directly created us to be who we are, disabilities and physical flaws and all. We need to learn the perspective of George MacDonald: "I would rather be what God chose to make me than the most glorious creature that I could think of. For to have been thought about—born in God's thoughts—and then made by God is the dearest, grandest, most precious thing in all thinking."[7]

If we have physical or mental disabilities or impairments, it is because God in His wisdom and love created us that way. We might not understand why God chose to do that, but that is where our trusting Him has to begin.

This truth can be difficult to accept, especially if you or a loved one is the object of such disability. But Jesus affirmed God's hand in disabilities. When the disciples asked Him why a certain man was born blind, He replied, "That the works of God might be displayed in him" (John 9:3).

That hardly seems fair, does it? Why should that man suffer blindness all those years merely to be available to display God's work on a certain day? Is God's glory worth a man's being born blind? And what about our own physical disabilities and inadequacies? Is God's glory worthy of those also? Are we willing to take our physical limitations, our learning disabilities, and even our appearance problems to God and say, "Father, You are worthy of this infirmity in my life. I believe that You created me just the way I am because You love me and want to glorify Yourself through me. I will trust You for who I am"?

This is the path to self-acceptance. And we must continually keep in mind that the God who created us the way we are is wise enough to know what's best for us and loving enough to bring it about. Certainly, we'll sometimes struggle with who we are. Our disabilities and infirmities are always with us, so we have to learn to trust God in this area continually.

Here again, James Hufstetler is helpful to us: "You will never really enjoy other people, you will never have stable emotions, you will never lead a life of godly contentment, you will never conquer jealousy and love others as you should until you thank God for making you the way he did."[8]

Paul once wrote, "What do you have that you did not receive?" (1 Corinthians 4:7). Let us learn to receive with thankfulness everything we have from God—disabilities as well as our so-called positive abilities—and seek to use them for His glory.

EVERYTHING PLANNED

*In your book were written, every one of them,
the days that were formed for me, when as
yet there was none of them.*

PSALM 139:16

When David speaks in Psalm 139:16 of how "the days that were formed for me" were already written in God's book, he may have meant that the span of his lifetime—his number of days on earth—had been divinely ordained by God. Certainly, this truth is stated elsewhere in Scripture. David said to God in 31:15, "My times are in your hand." Job confessed to God that each man's "days are determined; you have decreed the number of his months and have set limits he cannot exceed" (Job 14:5, NIV). And Paul declared that even for nations, God "marked out their appointed times in history" (Acts 17:26, NIV).

God has sovereignly determined how long each of us will live. This in itself is a glorious truth. Along with David, our times are in His hand. As one line from a song by John Ryland says, "Till He bids, I cannot die."

But it is likely that in Psalm 139:16, David had in mind a different meaning—that all the experiences of his life, day by day, were written down in God's book before he was even born. (This meaning fits better with the context in verses 13-15.) For all of us, this truth refers not simply to God's prior knowledge of what will occur in our lives but also to His plan for our lives.

It has been well said that one of the most inspiring of truths is that God has a distinct plan for each of us in sending us into this world. This plan embraces not only His original creation of us but also our family and the social setting into which we were born. It includes all the vicissitudes of life, all the seemingly chance or random happenings, and all the sudden and unexpected turns of events, both good and bad, that occur in our lives. All these situations and circumstances, though they may appear as only happenstance, were written in God's book before one of them came to be.

God created each of us uniquely to fulfill the plan He has ordained for us. Our disabilities as well as our abilities all fit into that plan. Did He create you with an incurable speech impediment? He did so because that particular infirmity uniquely fits you for the life He has planned for you. His plan for you and His creation of you were consistent. He equipped you to fulfill His specific purpose for you. God's plan for us fully embraces that which He wants us to be and do. God sovereignly determines our respective functions in the body of Christ and gives us the corresponding spiritual gifts with which to perform those functions (see Romans 12:4-6; 1 Corinthians 12:7-11). Moreover, our spiritual gifts are generally consistent with the physical and mental abilities as well as the temperaments with which God created us.

God doesn't look us over on the day we accept Christ and say, "Let's see, what spiritual gifts shall I give you?" No, God has planned our days before even one of them came to be. As He said to Jeremiah, "*Before I formed you in the womb* I knew you, and *before you were born* I consecrated you" (Jeremiah 1:5). Paul viewed his apostolic call in the same manner; he spoke of how God "set me apart before I was born, and . . . called me by his grace" (Galatians 1:15).

If there's one area of life where the saying "The grass is always greener on the other side of the fence" applies most, surely it's this area of vocational calling and station in life. Someone has estimated that as many as 80 percent of our workforce are dissatisfied with the jobs they're in. For many of us, that may be due to a reluctance to be what God planned for us to be.

But just as we must trust God for *who* we are, we must trust Him also for *what* we are, whether an engineer or a missionary, a homemaker or a nurse.

D

15

RESPONDING TO GOD'S PLAN

Whatever your hand finds to do, do it with your might.
ECCLESIASTES 9:10

Although I studied engineering in college, I soon left that vocation because I thought God wanted me to be an overseas missionary. But God never allowed me to become an overseas missionary. Instead, I became an administrator in a missions organization. At first I thought of administration as a temporary interlude on the way to the mission field. Then one day, I had to face the fact that God had gifted me both by talent and temperament for administration, and this was probably what He'd called me to do.

For a time, I thought of myself as a reluctant administrator, as one who would rather be out in the so-called "ministry." But I realized that such thoughts revealed a hesitation to accept God's plan for me. I had to realize He created me a certain way to fulfill a certain plan He'd ordained before I was born.

God determines the course of *all* our lives, for plumbers just as much as for pastors. That thought should give meaning to the most humdrum of vocations. In fact, no vocation should be considered humdrum if God has ordained it. In the words of J. R. Miller, "The question of small or great has no place here. To have been thought about at all, and then fashioned by God's hands to fill any place, is glory enough for the grandest and most aspiring life. And the highest place to which anyone can attain in life is that for which he was designed and made."[9]

This is not to deny that work, along with all other aspects of creation, is under the curse of sin (see Genesis 3:19). Becoming a Christian does not remove that curse from our respective jobs, but it should give us a new perspective about those jobs. We should begin to view them not as a necessary evil through which we eat our daily bread but rather as the place where God has placed us to serve Him by serving society. Addressing slaves, Paul wrote, "Whatever you do, work heartily, as for the Lord and not for men" (Colossians 3:23).

Undoubtedly, many of those believing slaves were assigned to irksome and wearisome tasks. Some were probably working far beneath their abilities or training. But they were to labor with enthusiasm because they were doing it for the Lord — doing the things ordained for them before they were born.

The realization that God has planned our days for us should not lead us to a fatalistic acceptance of the status quo. If we have the opportunity to improve our situation in a way that will honor God, we should do so. Even to believing slaves, Paul wrote, "If you can gain your freedom, avail yourself of the opportunity" (1 Corinthians 7:21). But immediately before that statement, he had written, "Were you a bondservant when called? Do not be concerned about it." Our lives demand a delicate balance between godly efforts to improve our situation and godly acceptance of those situations we cannot honorably change.

For most of us, our lives hold many seemingly adverse details that will not be changed regardless of our efforts or our prayers. They're simply part of God's plan. In such situations, we need to take comfort from the words of God to the Jewish captives in Babylon: "I know the plans I have for you, declares the LORD, plans for welfare and not for evil, to give you a future and a hope" (Jeremiah 29:11). Those words reveal God's heart for all His children. Just as He planned only good for those Jewish captives, so He plans only good for you and me.

The plan God ordained for you and wrote down in His book even before you were born is a good plan, not a harmful one. I readily acknowledge there are many aspects of His plan for each of us that do seem hurtful, that do seem calculated to take away hope. But here again, we are called to walk by faith, to trust God in the face of these adversities that will not go away.

GOD TAKES THE INITIATIVE

You shall remember the whole way that
the LORD your God has led you.
DEUTERONOMY 8:2

The realization that God has ordained our days for us leads us logically to think, *Can I trust God to guide me in that plan? What if I make a mistake and miss the way?* In answering such questions, I find it helpful to distinguish between God's guidance and that which has come to be called by such terms as "finding the will of God." We think so much about our responsibility to discover God's will in a situation (usually some "fork in the road" type of issue) or to make wise decisions in life's choices, but the biblical emphasis seems to be on God's faithfulness in guiding us.

David said of God, "He *leads* me beside still waters. . . . He *leads* me in paths of righteousness for his name's sake" (Psalm 23:2-3). The imagery is that of the shepherd guiding his sheep, and the initiative is with the shepherd. He's the one who determines the watering places and directs the flock as he thinks best. As our shepherd, God has committed Himself to guiding us in the ways He knows to be best for us. God sovereignly steers our lives so that we indeed live out in daily experience all the days ordained for us.

Consider, for example, the clear initiative expressed by God in these words of promise to His people through the prophet Isaiah:

> I will lead the blind
>   in a way that they do not know,
> in paths that they have not known
>   I will guide them.
> I will turn the darkness before them into light,
>   the rough places into level ground.
> These are the things I do,
>   and I do not forsake them. (Isaiah 42:16)

Thus says the LORD,
    your Redeemer, the Holy One of Israel:
"I am the LORD your God,
    who teaches you to profit,
    who leads you in the way you should go." (48:17)

His active, assured guidance is reflected as well in the words of Proverbs 4:11-12: "I have taught you the way of wisdom; I have led you in the paths of uprightness. When you walk, your step will not be hampered, and if you run, you will not stumble."

Consider also the book of Acts. The only reference to the disciples' seeking to determine the will of God occurs in the choosing of Matthias to succeed Judas. From that point onward, it is a record of God's guiding His people. In Acts 16, for example, Paul and his companions were moving ahead in their missionary journey in a logical progression. Twice, however, they were stopped by the Holy Spirit and then, as a result of Paul's vision, concluded that God was calling them to Macedonia. As they moved ahead, the Spirit guided them, stopping them in two places and calling them to another. The account doesn't tell us how the Spirit guided; it simply says that He did.

God did have a plan for Paul and his team that was more specific than the Great Commission to make disciples of all nations. The provinces of Asia and Bithynia that Paul was prevented from entering were just as needy as Macedonia. But it was God's plan that Paul should take the gospel to Macedonia and then to the entire Grecian peninsula. God did not leave it to Paul to seek His will. Rather, as Paul moved along, God took the initiative to guide him.

God does have a plan for each of us. He has given each of us different gifts, abilities, and temperaments and has placed each of us in the body of Christ according to His will. To thus place us in the body of Christ obviously denotes far more than leaving the choice to us; it means actually putting us there. It includes all the providential circumstances that are brought to bear upon us to ensure that we do find our rightful place in Christ's body and fulfill the functions He has given us to do.

CERTAIN GUIDANCE

Good and upright is the Lord; therefore
he instructs sinners in the way. He leads
the humble in what is right, and
teaches the humble his way.

Psalm 25:8-9

We do have a responsibility to make wise decisions, or discover the will of God (whichever term we may prefer to use), but God's plan for us is not contingent upon our decisions. God's plan is not contingent at all. God's plan is sovereign. It includes our foolish decisions as well as our wise ones.

For most of us, many of life's more crucial decisions are made before we have enough spiritual wisdom to make wise decisions. When I was a senior in college, I interviewed for and was offered a job to become effective upon completion of my required military service. At that time, I didn't know anything about the will of God or about making wise spiritual decisions. However, for some reason, I turned down the job. Looking back now, I can see that God was guiding me, keeping me available for His later call to The Navigators' ministry.

God's means of guidance are infinite. As I look back over the decades of my Christian life, I am amazed at the many and diverse ways by which God has guided me. I am inclined to say with David, "How precious to me are your thoughts, O God! How vast is the sum of them!" (Psalm 139:17). God is at work guiding all the details of my life.

Like most Christians, I've struggled over the right choice at some of those "fork in the road" decision points we encounter from time to time. I may have made some wrong decisions; I don't know. But God in His sovereignty has faithfully guided me in His path through right decisions and wrong ones. I'm where I am today not because I've always made wise decisions or correctly discovered the will of God at particular points along the way but because God has faithfully led me and guided me along the path of His will for me.

God's guidance is almost always step-by-step; He does not show us His plan for us all at once. Sometimes our anxiousness to know the will of God comes from a desire to "peer over God's shoulder" to see what His plan is. What we need to do is learn to trust Him to guide us.

Of course, this doesn't mean putting our minds into neutral and expecting God to guide us in some mysterious way apart from hard and prayerful thinking on our part. It does mean, as J. I. Packer has said, "God made us thinking beings, and he guides our minds as we think things out in his presence."[10]

I believe that Dr. Packer has expressed it so well: God guides our minds as we think. But the important truth is that God does guide. He does not play games with us. He does not look down from heaven at our struggles to know His will and say, "I hope you make the right decision." Rather, in His time and in His way, He will lead us along His path for us.

Many years ago, Fanny J. Crosby penned these words, which are so appropriate to this topic of trusting God for guidance:

> All the way my Savior leads me; what have I to ask beside?
> Can I doubt His tender mercy, who through life has been my
>   guide?
> Heavenly peace, divinest comfort, here by faith in Him to
>   dwell!
> For I know, whate'er befall me, Jesus doeth all things well.
> All the way my Savior leads me — O the fullness of His love!

Perfect rest to me is promised in my Father's house above.
When my spirit, clothed immortal, wings its flight to realms
of day,
This my song through endless ages: Jesus led me all the
way.[11]

We can trust God to guide us. He will lead us all the way. And when we stand before His throne, we will not be singing about successfully discovering the will of God; rather, we'll be rejoicing in how He led us all the way.

GOOD REASON TO WELCOME ADVERSITY

Count it all joy, my brothers, when you meet trials of various kinds.

JAMES 1:2

One of the many fascinating events in nature is the emergence of the cecropia moth from its cocoon, an event that occurs only with much struggle on the part of the moth to free itself. The story is frequently told of someone's trying to help a moth through its struggle by snipping the shell of the cocoon. The moth soon emerged with its wings crimped and shriveled and weak. In a few moments, the insect would have stretched those wings to fly but was now doomed to crawling out its brief life in frustration of never being the beautiful creature God created it to be. What the person in the story didn't realize was that the struggle to emerge from the cocoon is an essential part of developing the muscle system of the moth's body and pushing the body fluids out into the wings to expand them.

The adversities we face are much like the cocoon of the cecropia moth. God uses them to develop the spiritual "muscle system" of our lives.

As James wrote, we're to welcome adversity because "the testing of your faith produces steadfastness" (James 1:3), which in turn leads to maturity of our character.

We can be sure that the development of a beautiful Christlike character will not occur in our lives without adversity. Think of those lovely graces Paul calls the fruit of the Spirit in Galatians 5:22-23. The first four traits he mentions — love, joy, peace, and patience — can be developed only in the womb of adversity.

We may think we have true Christian love until someone offends us or treats us unjustly. Then we begin to see anger and resentment well up within us. We may conclude we have learned about genuine Christian joy until our lives are shattered by an unexpected calamity or grievous disappointment. Adversities spoil our peace and sorely try our patience. God uses those difficulties to reveal our need to grow so that we'll reach out to Him to change us more and more into the likeness of His Son.

Both Paul and James speak of rejoicing in our sufferings (see Romans 5:3-4; James 1:2-4). Most of us, if we're honest with ourselves, have difficulty with that idea. Endure them, perhaps, but rejoice? That often seems like an unreasonable expectation. We are not masochistic; we don't enjoy pain.

But Paul and James both say that we should rejoice in our trials because of their beneficial results. It's not the adversity considered in itself that is to be the grounds for our joy; rather, it is the expectation of the results—the development of our character—that should cause us to rejoice in adversity. God does not ask us to rejoice because we have lost our job or a loved one has been stricken with cancer or a child has been born with an incurable birth defect. But He does tell us to rejoice because we believe He's in control of those circumstances and is at work through them for our ultimate good.

However, we shrink from adversity. To return to the moth illustration, we want God to snip the cocoon of adversity we often find ourselves in and release us. But He has more wisdom and love for us than we do for ourselves. He will not remove the adversity until we have profited from it and developed in whatever way He intended in bringing or allowing it into our lives.

The Christian life is intended to be one of continuous growth. We all want to grow, but we often resist the process, focusing on the adversity itself rather than looking beyond it with the eye of faith to what God is doing in our lives.

It was said of Jesus that He "for the joy that was set before him endured the cross, despising the shame" (Hebrews 12:2). As that passage further states, we're to fix our eyes on Him and follow His example, rejoicing in how God is at work in us to cause us to grow.

A WORK THAT WILL
BE COMPLETED

Blessed is the man whom you discipline, O Lord,
and whom you teach out of your law.

PSALM 94:12

God doesn't ask us how or when we want to grow. He's the Master Teacher, training His pupils when and how He deems best.

Both the Hebrew and Greek languages express *discipline* and *teaching* by the same word. God intends that we grow through the disciplines of adversity as well as through instruction from His Word.

One of the most encouraging passages in the Bible is

Philippians 1:6: "I am sure of this, that he who began a good work in you will bring it to completion at the day of Jesus Christ." He will not fail to finish the training that He has begun in us. He's committed to "working in us that which is pleasing in his sight" (Hebrews 13:21). As Horatius Bonar wrote, "God's treatment must succeed. It cannot miscarry or be frustrated even in its most arduous efforts, even in reference to its minutest objects. It is the mighty power of God that is at work within us and upon us, and this is our consolation. . . . All is love, all is wisdom, and all is faithfulness, yet all is also power."[12]

That God cannot fail in His purpose for adversity in our lives, that He will accomplish that which He intends, is a great encouragement to me. Sometimes I fail to respond to difficulties in a God-honoring way, but my failure doesn't mean God has failed. Even my painfully sharp awareness of failure may be used of God (for example, to help me grow in humility). And perhaps that was God's intention all along.

God knows what He's doing. Again in the words of Bonar, "He knows exactly what we need and how to supply it. . . . His training is no random work. It is carried on with exquisite skill."[13] God knows us better than we know ourselves and knows unerringly where we need to grow. He carries on His work with a skill that far exceeds that of the most expert physician. He correctly diagnoses our need and applies the most-sure remedy.

If any adversity coming across our path were not beneficial, God would not allow it or send it: "He does not willingly bring affliction or grief to anyone" (Lamentations 3:33, NIV). God does not delight in our suffering. He brings only that which is necessary, but He does not shrink from that which will help us grow.

Because He's so sovereignly at work in our lives through adversity, we must learn to respond to what He's doing. His sovereign work never negates our responsibility. Just as God teaches us through adversity, we must seek to learn from it.

To learn from adversity and receive the beneficial effects God intends, we can first submit to it—not reluctantly, as the defeated warrior submits to his conqueror, but voluntarily, as the patient on the operating table submits to the skilled hand of the surgeon. Don't try to frustrate the gracious purpose of God by resisting His providence in your life. Rather, insofar as you're able to see what God is doing, make His purpose your purpose.

This doesn't mean we shouldn't use all legitimate means at our disposal to minimize adversity's effects. It means we should accept from God's hand the success or failure of those means as He wills and at all times seek to learn whatever He might be teaching us.

Sometimes we'll perceive quite clearly what God is doing, and in those instances, we should respond to God's teaching in humble obedience. At other times, we may not be able to see at all what He's doing. At those times, we should respond in humble faith, trusting Him to work out in our lives that which we need to learn. Both attitudes are important, and God wants one at one time and the other at another time.

GOD'S WORD IN
MY ADVERSITY

*The commandment is a lamp and
the teaching a light, and the
reproofs of discipline are
the way of life.*
PROVERBS 6:23

To profit most from adversity, we have to bring the Word of God to bear upon our situation. We should ask God to bring to our attention pertinent passages of Scripture and then look for those passages.

My first great lesson on the sovereignty of God is still stamped indelibly on my mind after many years. It came as

I was desperately searching the Scriptures to find some kind of an answer to a severe time of testing.

As we do this, we'll find we not only profit from the circumstances themselves but also gain new insight into the Scriptures. Martin Luther reportedly said, "Were it not for tribulation, I should not understand the Scriptures." Although we may be going to the Scriptures to learn how to respond to our adversities, we find those adversities in turn help us understand the Scriptures. It is not that we will learn from adversity something different than what we can learn from the Scriptures. Rather, adversity enhances the teaching of God's Word and makes it more profitable to us. In some instances, it clarifies our understanding and causes us to see truths we had passed over before. At other times, it will transform "head knowledge" into "heart knowledge" as theological theory becomes a reality to us.

The Puritan Daniel Dyke said,

Look not for any new diverse doctrine to be taught thee by affliction, which is not in the word. For in truth, herein stands our teaching by affliction, that it fits and prepares us for the word, by breaking and sub-dividing the stubbornness of our hearts, and making them pliable, and capable of the impression of the word.[14]

We might say, then, that the Word of God and adversity have a synergistic effect as God uses both of them together to bring about growth in our lives that neither the Word nor adversity would accomplish by itself.

To further profit from our adversities, we must also consistently remember them and recall the lessons we have learned from them. God wants us to do more than simply endure our trials, even more than merely find comfort in them; He wants us to remember them, and not just as trials or sorrows but as His disciplines—His means of bringing about growth in our lives.

In Deuteronomy 8:3, Moses told the Israelites, "[God] humbled you and let you hunger and fed you with manna . . . that he might make you know that man does not live by bread alone, but man lives by every word that comes from the mouth of the Lord." (The "word . . . from the mouth of the Lord" in this passage is not Scripture but the word of God's providence; see Psalm 33:6,9 and 148:5 for similar usage.) God wanted to teach the Israelites that they were dependent upon Him for their daily bread. He did this by bringing adversity in the form of hunger into their lives. But in order to profit from this lesson, they were commanded to remember it: "And you shall remember the whole way that the Lord your God has led you" (Deuteronomy 8:2).

If we too are to profit from the painful lessons God teaches us, we must remember them.

I once learned a rather painful lesson after trying to subtly usurp some of God's glory for my own reputation. God holds me responsible to remember that lesson. Every time I come across God's words in Isaiah 42:8, "My glory I give to no other," in either my Bible reading or my Scripture memory review, I should remember that painful circumstance and let the lesson sink more deeply into my heart. Every time I stand up to teach God's Word, I should remember that lesson and purge my heart of any desire to enhance my own reputation. This is the way adversity becomes profitable to us.

DAY

21

FOR FRUITFULNESS AND HOLINESS

*Every branch that does bear fruit he prunes,
that it may bear more fruit.*

JOHN 15:2

In John 15, Jesus pictures God as a master gardener who prunes the branches of His vineyard. Every healthy vine requires both nourishment and pruning. Through the Word of God, we're nourished (see Psalm 1:2-3), but through adversity, we're pruned.

Jesus speaks at length in this passage of how God prunes every fruit-bearing branch so it will be even more fruitful. In the natural realm, pruning is important for fruit bearing.

An unpruned vine will produce a great deal of unproductive growth but little fruit; cutting away unwanted and useless growth forces the plant to use its life to produce fruit.

So also in the spiritual realm, God must prune us. As believers, we still have a sinful nature, and we tend to pour our spiritual energies into that which is not true fruit. We seek position, success, and reputation even in the body of Christ. We depend upon natural talents and human wisdom. And we're easily distracted and pulled by the things of the world—its pleasures and possessions.

God uses adversity to loosen our grip on those things that are not true fruit. A severe illness, the death of someone dear to us, the loss of material substance, the tarnishing of our reputation, the turning aside of friends, or the dashing of our cherished dreams on the rocks of failure—any of those things can cause us to reassess what is really important in our lives. After experiencing such difficulties, position or possessions or even reputation no longer seems so important. We begin to relinquish our desires and expectations—even good ones—to the sovereign will of God. We come more and more to depend on God and to desire only that which will count for eternity. God is pruning us so we will be more fruitful.

We often resist this work of God in our lives. But as we look to Him, we may be sure to see how in due time His discipline "yields the peaceful fruit of righteousness to those who have been trained by it" (Hebrews 12:11).

The pruning, disciplinary work of adversity also causes us to grow in holiness: "He disciplines us for our good, that we may share his holiness" (verse 10). How exactly does this happen?

For one thing, adversity reveals the corruption of our sinful nature. We don't know ourselves or the depths of sin remaining in us. We agree with Scripture's teachings and assume that agreement means obedience. At least we intend to obey.

Who of us doesn't read that list of Christian virtues called "the fruit of the Spirit"—"love, joy, peace, patience, kindness, goodness, faithfulness, gentleness, self-control" (Galatians 5:22-23)—and agree we want all those traits in our lives? We even begin to think we are making good progress in growing in them.

But then adversity comes. We find we're unable to love, from the depths of our heart, the person who's the instrument of the adversity. We're not disposed to trust God; unbelief and resentment surge within us. We're dismayed at the scene. Our growth in Christian character seems to vanish like a vapor. We feel as if we're back in spiritual kindergarten. But through this experience, God has revealed to us some of the remaining corruption within us.

"Blessed," Jesus said, "are the poor in spirit . . . those who mourn . . . those who hunger and thirst for righteousness" (Matthew 5:3-4,6). These descriptions refer to the believer who has been humbled over his sinfulness, mourns because of it, and yearns with all his heart for God to change him. But no one adopts this attitude without being exposed to the evil and corruption of his own heart. God uses adversity to do this.

In making us holy, God wants to get at the root corruption of our sinful nature. He uses adversity to enlighten our minds about our own needs as well as the teachings of Scripture. He uses adversity to rein in our affections that have been drawn out to unholy desires and subdue our stubborn and rebellious wills.

FOR GREATER DEPENDENCE

I am the vine; you are the branches. Whoever
abides in me and I in him, he it is that bears
much fruit, for apart from me you
can do nothing.
JOHN 15:5

God must continually be at work on our tendency to rely on ourselves instead of on Him. Apart from our union with Christ and a total reliance upon Him, we can do nothing that glorifies God. We live in a world that worships independence and self-reliance, and because of our own sinful nature, we can easily fall into the world's pattern of thinking. God has to teach us through adversity to rely on Him instead of our own business acumen, our ministry experience, and even our goodness and morality.

The apostle Paul described a time when he and his band of men were "utterly burdened beyond our strength" (2 Corinthians 1:8); he saw, however, the higher purpose in this: "to make us rely not on ourselves but on God who raises the dead" (verse 9). They had nowhere to turn except to God.

Paul had to learn dependence on God in the spiritual as well as the physical realm. His "thorn in the flesh" (see 12:7) was an adversity he desperately wanted to be rid of. But God let it remain, not only to curb any tendency for pride in Paul's heart but also to teach him to rely on God's strength. Paul had to learn that it was not his strength but God's grace — God's enabling power — that he must depend on.

Paul was one of the most brilliant men in history, with an abundance of natural intellect. God also gave him divine revelations, some so glorious that Paul wasn't permitted to tell about them. But God never allowed Paul to depend on either his intellect or his revelations. He had to depend on God's grace, just as you and I do, and he learned this through severe adversity.

If God is going to use you and me, He will bring adversity into our lives so that we too may learn experientially our dependence on Him.

I am a person of many weaknesses and few natural strengths. My physical limitations, though not apparent to most people, prevent my relating to other men through golf, tennis, or other recreational sports. I feel this keenly, and for some years I wrestled frequently with God about it. But I have at last concluded that my weaknesses are actually channels for His strength. After many years, I think I am finally at the point where I can say with Paul, "I am content with weaknesses. . . . For when I am weak, then I am strong" (2 Corinthians 12:10).

It really doesn't matter how many strengths or weaknesses you possess on the natural level. You may be the most competent person in your field, but you can be sure that if God is going to use you, He will cause you to feel keenly your dependence on Him. He will often blight the very thing we feel confident in so that we will learn to depend on Him, not on ourselves. According to Stephen, "Moses was educated in all the wisdom of the Egyptians and was powerful in speech and action" (Acts 7:22, NIV); moreover, he "thought that his own people would realize that God was using him to rescue them" (verse 25, NIV). But when Moses attempted to take matters into his own hands, God so frustrated his efforts that Moses had to flee for his life. Forty years later, he still had no confidence in his own abilities and even had difficulty believing that God could use him.

Paul experienced a thorn in the flesh. Moses saw his efforts to do something for God utterly frustrated and turned into disaster.

Each of these men of God experienced an adversity that caused him to realize his own weakness and his dependence on God. Each adversity was different, but the men had a common goal of bringing God's servants to a place of greater dependence on God. This is also His goal with us.

PERSEVERANCE AND FAITH

You have need of endurance, so that when you have done the will of God you may receive what is promised.

HEBREWS 10:36

Perseverance is the quality of character that enables one to pursue a goal in spite of obstacles and difficulties. It's one thing to simply bear up under adversity. This in itself is commendable. But the Christian life is meant to be active, not passive. We're called to diligently pursue God's will. He calls us to do more than simply bear the load of adversity; He calls us to persevere (to press forward) in the face of it. He wants all Christians to finish well. He wants us to "run with endurance" (Hebrews 12:1).

Each of us has been given a race to run, a will of God to do. Along the way, all of us encounter innumerable obstacles and occasions for discouragement. God wants us to persist in doing His will whatever those obstacles might be. How can we do it?

Both Paul and James gave the same answer. Paul said, "Suffering produces perseverance" (Romans 5:3, NIV); James added, "The testing of your faith produces steadfastness" (James 1:3). We see here a mutually enhancing effect. Adversity produces perseverance, and perseverance enables us to meet adversity. A good analogy is found in weight training. Lifting weights develops muscle, and the more one's muscles are developed, the heavier the weight one can lift.

Though perseverance is developed in the crucible of adversity, it is energized by faith. Again, consider the analogy of weight training. Although the weights on a bar provide the resistance needed to develop muscle, they do not provide the energy. That must come from within the athlete's body. In the case of adversity, the energy must come from God through faith. It is His strength, not ours, that enables us to persevere, and we lay hold of His strength through faith.

It has often been observed that the Christian life is not a sprint but a marathon. Even those metaphors fail to adequately express reality. The Christian life could better be described as an obstacle course of marathon length. Think of a race course just over twenty-six miles in length. Add to it walls to climb over, streams to forge, hedges to jump across, and an endless variety of other unexpected obstacles. That is the Christian life, and it has prompted the observation that few Christians finish well.

But God wants *all* Christians to finish well. He wants us to run with perseverance, persistently doing His will whatever the obstacles.

William Carey, often called the father of modern missions, is a famous example of one who persevered. Despite a succession of unbelievable obstacles (including an unsympathetic wife who later became insane), he translated all or parts of the Bible into forty languages and dialects of India. His sister is equally an example of one who persevered; almost totally paralyzed and bedridden, she lay on her bed in London and prayed for all the details and struggles of her brother's work in far-off India.

Few people can identify with William Carey's perseverance in either the obstacles he faced or the amazing tasks he accomplished. But we should identify with the perseverance of Carey's sister, who persevered in doing God's will as an invalid. She could not do much (as we tend to think of it), but she persevered in doing what she could. And because she persevered in prayer, her brother was strengthened and enabled to persevere in his missionary labors in India. Carey's sister did more than bear cheerfully her paralysis; she persevered in doing the will of God in spite of it.

Sandwiched between strong calls for perseverance at Hebrews 10:36 and 12:1 is the well-known chapter on faith, Hebrews 11. This motivational chapter is calling us to persevere by faith, as we're shown example after example of people who persevered in doing God's will by trusting Him. It's by faith that we're called to persevere — doing God's will despite the obstacles and discouragements, and always in His strength and His alone.

GOING DEEPER
WITH GOD

*You have tried my heart, you have visited
me by night, you have tested me.*

PSALM 17:3

Perhaps the most valuable way we profit from adversity is in
the deepening of our relationship with God. Through adversity, we learn to bow before His sovereignty, trust His wisdom,
and experience the consolations of His love. We can say with
Job, "I had heard of you by the hearing of the ear, but now my
eye sees you" (Job 42:5). We begin to pass from knowing
about God to knowing God Himself in a personal and
intimate way.

In Philippians 3:10, Paul speaks of the fellowship of sharing in the suffering of Jesus Christ—that is, of believers sharing with our Lord in His suffering. Paul's goal, he declares, is this: "that I may know him and the power of his resurrection, and may share his sufferings, becoming like him in his death." Down through the centuries, this verse has given expression to the deepest heart cry of believers: the desire to know Christ in an ever-increasing, intimate, personal way.

I can remember as a young Christian being challenged to "know Christ and to make Him known," and I can remember praying, because of Philippians 3:10, that God would enable me to know Christ more and more. I have to confess, though, that deep inside, it always bothered me a bit that Paul wanted not only to know Christ Himself but also to experience the fellowship of His suffering. To know Christ in a more intimate way and to experience the power of His resurrection in my life appealed to me, but not the suffering. I shrank from that.

I've come to see, however, that the message of Philippians 3:10 is a package deal. Part of coming to know Christ in a more intimate way is through the fellowship of His suffering. If we're to truly grow in knowing Christ, to experience the power of His resurrection, we can be sure we'll face the fellowship of His suffering to some degree.

The suffering Paul envisions here is not limited to persecution for the sake of the gospel. It includes all adversity that overtakes the believer and has conformity to Christ as its ultimate purpose, described here by Paul as "becoming like him in his death."

Repeatedly in the Bible, we see men and women of God drawn into a deeper relationship with Him through adversity. There's no doubt that all the circumstances in the long delay of the birth of Isaac and then the experience of taking his only son up to the mountain to offer as a sacrifice brought Abraham into a much deeper relationship with God. The Psalms are replete with expressions of ever-deepening knowledge of God as the psalmists seek Him in times of adversity (see Psalms 23; 42; 61–62).

You and I obviously do not seek out adversity just so we can develop a deeper relationship with God. Rather God, through adversity, seeks us out. He draws us more and more into a deeper relationship with Him. If we're seeking Him, it's because He's seeking us. One of the strong cords with which He draws us closer is adversity. If we'll seek to cooperate with God, we'll find that we'll be drawn into a deeper relationship with Him. We'll come to know Him as Abraham and Job and David and Paul came to know Him.

As we experience God's seeking of us through adversity, sometimes we'll be able to see how we are profiting from it, while at other times we'll wonder what God is doing. One thing we may be sure of, however: For the believer, all pain has meaning; all adversity is profitable.

There's no question that adversity is difficult. It usually takes us by surprise and seems to strike where we're most vulnerable. It often appears completely senseless and irrational; but to God, none of it is either senseless or irrational. He has a purpose in every pain He brings or allows in our lives. We can be sure that in some way He intends it for our profit and His glory.

CHOOSING TO TRUST GOD

Why are you cast down, O my soul, and
why are you in turmoil within me? Hope
in God; for I shall again praise him,
my salvation and my God.

PSALM 42:11

In times of distress, David *chose* to trust God, even while admitting fear. He said,

When I am afraid,
    I put my trust in you.
In God, whose word I praise,

in God I trust; I shall not be afraid.
What can flesh do to me? (Psalm 56:3-4)

Although he was a warrior of great skill and courage, there were times when David was afraid. The heading of this psalm indicates the occasion of David's writing: "When the Philistines seized him in Gath." The historical narrative of that incident says that "David . . . was *much afraid* of Achish the king of Gath" (1 Samuel 21:12). Despite this fear, he affirmed to God his decision to trust Him and not be afraid.

Repeatedly in the Psalms, we find this determination to trust God despite all appearances. David's declaration in Psalm 23:4, "I will fear no evil," is equivalent to "I will trust in God in the face of evil." In 16:8, he said, "I have set the LORD always before me; because he is at my right hand, I shall not be shaken." To "set the Lord before me" is to recognize His presence and constant help, something we must *choose* to do.

God is always with us. He has said, "Never will I leave you; never will I forsake you" (Hebrews 13:5, NIV). There's no question of His presence with us, but we must *recognize* His presence, setting Him always before us. We must choose whether to believe His promises of constant protection and care.

In speaking of how we may come to accept adversity in our lives, Margaret Clarkson wrote, "Always it is initiated by an act of will on our part; we set ourselves to believe in the overruling goodness, providence, and sovereignty of God and refuse to turn aside no matter what may come, no matter how we feel."[15]

For many years in my own pilgrimage of seeking to trust God at all times (I'm still far from the end of that journey), I was a prisoner to my feelings. I mistakenly thought that I couldn't trust God unless I *felt* like trusting Him (which I almost never did in times of adversity). Now I'm learning that trusting God is first of all a matter of the will and not dependent on my feelings. I choose to trust God, and my feelings eventually follow.

Let me add that choosing to trust God is a matter of knowledge. We must *know* that He is sovereign, wise, and loving in all the ways we come to see in Scripture. The whole idea of trusting God is based upon the knowable fact that God *is* absolutely trustworthy. But having been exposed to the knowledge of this truth, we must then choose whether to believe what He has revealed to us rather than follow our feelings.

Choosing to trust God in this way in times of adversity is admittedly a hard thing to do. I don't mean to suggest that the choice is as easy as deciding whether to run to the store or even whether to do some compassionate deed. Trusting God is a matter of faith, and faith is the fruit of the Spirit (see

Galatians 5:22); only the Holy Spirit can make His Word come alive in our hearts and create faith. But we can choose to look to Him to do just that rather than be ruled by feelings of anxiety or resentment or grief.

David said, "I sought the LORD, and he answered me and delivered me from all my fears" (Psalm 34:4). There's no conflict between his affirming "I shall not be afraid" and his asking God to deliver him from fear. David recognized his responsibility to choose to trust God and also his need to depend on the Lord for the ability to do it.

IN HIS CONSTANT CARE

He has said, "I will never leave you nor forsake you."
HEBREWS 13:5

God's promise in Hebrews 13:5 includes five grammatical negatives in Greek, a force difficult to fully express in normal English. Some attempts include these: "I will never, never let go your hand: I will never, never forsake you"; "No, I will not leave, no, nor forsake thee"; "I will not, I will not, I will not in any degree leave you helpless nor forsake nor let you down."[16]

God wants us to firmly grasp the truth that whatever circumstances may indicate, we must believe, on the basis of

His promise, that He has not forsaken us or left us to the mercy of those circumstances.

We never lose God's presence and help, but we may sometimes lose the sense of them. Job, in his distress, could not find God. He said, "Behold, I go forward, but he is not there, and backward, but I do not perceive him; on the left hand when he is working, I do not behold him; he turns to the right hand, but I do not see him" (Job 23:8-9). Then he added, "But he knows the way that I take; when he has tried me, I shall come out as gold" (verse 10). Job apparently wavered, as we do, between trust and doubt. Here he said he couldn't find God anywhere; God had completely withdrawn the comforting sense of His presence. But though he couldn't see Him, Job believed that God was watching over him and would bring him through that trial as purified gold.

You and I will sometimes have the same experience as Job—perhaps not in the same kind or intensity of suffering, but in the seeming inability to find God anywhere. God will seem to hide Himself from us. Even the prophet Isaiah said to God on one occasion, "Truly, you are a God who hides himself, O God of Israel, the Savior" (Isaiah 45:15).

We should learn from Job and Isaiah so that we are not totally surprised and dismayed when, in the time of our distress, we can't seem to find God. At these times, we must cling to His bare but inviolate promise "I will never leave you nor forsake you."

The apostle Paul reminds us that "God . . . never lies" (Titus 1:2). This is the God who has promised, "I will never leave you nor forsake you." God may hide Himself from our sense of His presence, but He never allows our adversities to hide us from Him. He may allow us to pass through the deep waters and the fire, but He will be with us in them (see Isaiah 43:2).

Because God will never leave you nor forsake you, you're invited in the words of Peter to humble yourself under God's mighty hand, "casting all your anxieties on him, because he cares for you" (1 Peter 5:6-7). God cares for you! He's not just there with you; He cares for you.

His care is constant, not occasional or sporadic. His care is total; even the very hairs of your head are numbered. His care is sovereign; nothing can touch you that He does not allow. His care is infinitely wise and good so that, in the words of John Newton, "if it were possible for [us] to alter any part of his plan, [we] could only spoil it."[17]

We must learn to cast our anxieties on Him. Dr. John Brown said of this verse, "The figurative expression 'cast,' not lay, seems to intimate that the duty enjoined is one that requires an effort; and experience tells us it is no easy matter to throw off the burden of carefulness."[18] So we're back to the matter of choice. We must—by an act of the will, in dependence on the Holy Spirit—say something such as, "Lord, I choose to cast off this anxiety onto You, but I cannot do this of myself. I will trust You by Your Spirit to enable me, having cast my anxiety on You, not to take it back upon myself."

Trust is not a passive state of mind. It is a vigorous act of the soul by which we choose to lay hold of the promises of God and cling to them despite the adversity that at times seeks to overwhelm us.

MY STRONG TOWER

*I will say to the LORD, "My refuge and my
fortress, my God, in whom I trust."*
PSALM 91:2

Though we may earnestly seek to trust God in our larger
crisis experiences, we often try to work through life's minor
difficulties ourselves. Disposed as we are to trust in ourselves,
it sometimes takes a major crisis to turn us toward the Lord.
If, however, we learn to trust Him in minor adversities, we'll
be better prepared to trust Him in major ones. A mark of
Christian maturity is to continually trust the Lord in the
minutiae of daily life.

Several years ago, I encountered a series of related difficulties within a few days—not major calamities, but of a

nature as to cause me great distress. At the outset, the verse Psalm 50:15 came to my mind: "Call upon me in the day of trouble; I will deliver you, and you shall glorify me." I began to call upon God, asking Him to deliver me, but it seemed the more I called, the more the difficulties came.

I began to wonder if God's promises had any real meaning. Finally one day I said to God, "I will take You at Your Word. I will believe that in Your time and in Your way, You will deliver me." The difficulties did not cease, but the peace of God did quiet my fears and anxieties. And then, in due time, God did deliver me from those troubles, and He did it in such a way that I knew He had done it.

We also have a tendency to trust in God's instruments of provision rather than in God Himself. In the usual course of our lives, He provides for our needs through human means rather than directly. He provides for our financial needs through our vocations and gives us medical personnel to treat us when we're ill. But these human instruments are ultimately under God's controlling hand. They succeed only to the extent God prospers them. We must be careful to look beyond the means and human instrumentalities to the God who uses them.

In Proverbs 18:10-11, we find an interesting contrast drawn between the righteous and the rich: "The name of the Lord is a strong tower; the righteous man runs into it and is safe. A rich man's wealth is his strong city, and like a high wall in his imagination." The contrast is not between the righteous and the rich in an absolute sense, as there are many people who are both righteous and wealthy. The contrast, rather, is between the two primary objects of man's trust: God and money. Those who trust in the Lord are safe; those who trust in their wealth only *imagine* they're safe.

There's a much wider principle for us in this passage. All of us tend to have our imagined "strong city" with its "high walls." It may be an advanced college degree with its ticket to a guaranteed position, or our insurance policies, or our financial nest egg for retirement. For our nation, it's our military buildup. Anything other than God Himself that we tend to trust in becomes our fortified city with its imagined unscalable walls.

I don't mean to say we're to disregard the usual means of supply God provides; I'm saying that we're not to trust in them.

When the psalmist said, "Not in my bow do I trust, nor can my sword save me" (Psalm 44:6), he did not then add, "I've therefore thrown these weapons away." The proper perspective is to look to God and trust *Him* to use whatever means He has provided.

Human means and instrumentalities can be depended upon only insofar as we recognize and honor God in them.

And He is able to work with or without them. Though He most often uses human means, He is not dependent upon them and will frequently use some means altogether different from that which we would have expected. In fact, it seems from experience that God delights in surprising us by His ways of deliverance to remind us that our trust must be in Him and Him alone.

IN GOOD TIMES
AND BAD

*Trust in the L*ORD *forever, for the L*ORD
*G*OD *is an everlasting rock.*
ISAIAH 26:4

As hard as it is to trust God in times of adversity, there are
other times when it may be even harder, and that is when our
circumstances are going well. These are the times when, to
use David's expression, "the lines have fallen for me in pleasant places" (Psalm 16:6). At such times, we're prone to put
our trust in our blessings or, even worse, in ourselves as the
providers of those blessings.

During times of prosperity and favorable circumstances,

we show our trust in God by acknowledging Him as the provider of all those blessings. We can remember how God caused the nation of Israel to hunger in the desert and then fed them with manna from heaven in order to teach them "that man does not live by bread alone, but man lives by every word that comes from the mouth of the LORD" (Deuteronomy 8:3).

When our cupboards and refrigerators are filled with food for next week's meals, we're just as dependent upon God as the Israelites were. God rained down manna for them each day, providing their food through a miracle. For us, He may provide a regular paycheck and plenty of food at the supermarket ready to buy. He provides our food through a long and complex chain of natural events in which His hand is visible only to the eye of faith. But it's still just as much His provision as the manna from heaven was.

How often are our expressions of thanksgiving at mealtimes hardly more than a perfunctory ritual with little genuine feeling? How often do we stop to acknowledge God's hand of provision and thank Him for other temporal blessings: the clothes we wear, the house we live in, the car we drive, the health we enjoy? Genuinely thanking God for His blessings is an indicator of our trust in Him. We ought to be as earnest and frequent in our prayers of thanksgiving when the cupboard is full as we would be in our pleas of supplication if the cupboards were bare. That's how we show our trust in times of prosperity and blessing.

Solomon said, "In the day of prosperity be joyful, and in the day of adversity consider: God has made the one as well as the other" (Ecclesiastes 7:14). God makes the good times as well as the bad. In adversity we tend to doubt God's fatherly care, while in prosperity we tend to forget it.

Philip Bennett Power wrote,

> The daily circumstances of life will afford us opportunities enough of glorifying God in Trust, without our waiting for any extraordinary calls upon our faith. Let us remember that the extraordinary circumstances of life are but few; that much of life may slip past without their occurrence; and that if we be not faithful and trusting in that which is little, we are not likely to be so in that which is great. . . . Let our trust be reared in the humble nursery of our own daily experience, with its ever recurring little wants, and trials, and sorrows; and then, when need be, it will come forth, to do such great things as are required of it.[19]

If we're to trust God, we must acknowledge our dependence upon Him at all times, good times as well as bad, and in times of minor irritations as well as major hardship.

I once asked a dear saint of God who had experienced much adversity whether she found it as difficult to trust God in the minor troubles of life as in the major ones. She replied that she found the minor ones more difficult. In times of major crisis, she readily realized her utter dependence on God and quickly turned to Him, but she often tried to work through the more ordinary adversities herself. Let's learn from her experience and seek to trust God in all the circumstances of our lives.

THANKSGIVING FOLLOWS TRUST

*Give thanks in all circumstances; for this
is the will of God in Christ Jesus for you.*
1 Thessalonians 5:18

In our trusting God, there's more at stake than experiencing peace in the midst of difficulties or even deliverance from them. The honor of God should be our chief concern. Therefore, our primary response to the trustworthiness of God should be, "I will trust God." But there are some corollary responses to trusting Him that are also important. They provide tangible evidence that we are in fact trusting God. The foremost of these is thanksgiving.

Thanksgiving is not a natural virtue but rather a fruit of the Spirit, given by Him. One of the most indicting statements in the Bible about natural man is Paul's charge that "although they knew God, they did not honor him as God or *give thanks to him*" (Romans 1:21). The unbeliever isn't inclined to give thanks. If he sees life as anything beyond chance, he may congratulate himself for his successes and blame others for his failures, but he never sees and acknowledges the hand of God in his life.

In his gospel, Luke tells the story of ten lepers who were healed by Christ (see Luke 17:11-19). All ten cried out to be healed and actually experienced Christ's healing power, but only one came back to thank Jesus. How prone we are to be as the other nine, quick to ask for God's help but forgetful to give Him thanks.

In fact, our problem is far deeper than mere forgetfulness. We're imbued with a spirit of ingratitude because of our sinful nature. We must cultivate a new spirit, the spirit of gratitude, which the Holy Spirit has implanted within us at our salvation.

Thanksgiving is an admission of dependence. Through it, we recognize that in the physical realm, God "gives to all mankind life and breath and everything" (Acts 17:25), while in the spiritual realm, we recognize how God, "when we were dead in our trespasses, made us alive together with Christ"

(Ephesians 2:5). Everything we are and have we owe to His bountiful grace. "What do you have that you did not receive?" (1 Corinthians 4:7).

When Paul exhorts us to thanksgiving "in all circumstances" (1 Thessalonians 5:18), the literal translation of that phrase is "in everything." Thus, we see the close connection between this command and the promise of Romans 8:28; we're to give thanks in everything because "we know that for those who love God *all things* work together for good."

The basis for giving thanks in the difficult circumstances is what we learn about God in Scripture—His sovereignty, wisdom, and love—as they're brought to bear upon all the unexpected and sudden shifts and turns in our lives. In short, it's the firm belief that God is at work for our good in absolutely all our circumstances. It's the willingness to accept this truth from God's Word and rely upon it without having to know just how He is working for our good.

To derive the fullest comfort and encouragement from this truth, we must realize that God is at work in a preactive, not reactive, fashion. God does not just respond to an adversity in our lives to make the best of a bad situation. He knows before He initiates or permits the adversity exactly how He will use it for our good.

For example, God knew exactly what He was doing before He allowed Joseph's brothers to sell him into slavery. Joseph recognized this when he said much later to his brothers, "So it was not you who sent me here, but God. . . . You meant evil against me, but God meant it for good" (Genesis 45:8; 50:20).

That is why we're always to give thanks in whatever situation we find ourselves. It's another response to the trustworthiness of God. If we trust Him to work in all our circumstances for our good, then we should give Him thanks in all those circumstances—thanksgiving not for the evil considered in itself but for the good that He will bring out of that evil through His sovereign wisdom and love.

RESPONDING IN HUMILITY AND WORSHIP

Humble yourselves before the Lord,
and he will exalt you.

JAMES 4:10

Genuine trust in God prompts our worship of Him, even in hard times. When disaster struck Job, he "fell on the ground and worshiped. And he said, 'Naked I came from my mother's womb, and naked shall I return. The LORD gave, and the LORD has taken away; blessed be the name of the LORD'" (Job 1:20-21). Instead of raising his fist in God's face, Job prostrated himself in worship. Instead of defiance, there was a humble recognition of God's sovereignty: God had given; He had a right to take away.

Job was demonstrating a big part of the response that God, many centuries later, would command for us: "Humble yourselves, therefore, under the mighty hand of God . . . casting all your anxieties on him, because he cares for you" (1 Peter 5:6-7). We're to humbly submit to God's "mighty hand" — His sovereign dealings with us — while casting our anxieties on Him, convinced of His care. These anxieties, of course, arise out of the adversities God brings into our lives; we're to accept the adversities but not the anxieties. Our tendency is exactly the opposite: We seek to escape from or resist adversities, all the while clinging to the anxieties they produce.

Humility should be both a response to adversity and a fruit of it. Paul was clear that the primary purpose of the "thorn" in his flesh was to curb his tendency toward pride (see 2 Corinthians 12:7). If Paul tended to be prideful, surely we do also. Therefore, we can expect that whenever God blesses us in any way that might engender our pride, He'll also give us a "thorn in the flesh" to oppose and undermine that pride. We'll be made weak in some way through one or more adversities so that we might recognize that our strength is in Him, not in ourselves.

We may chafe under such thorn, or we can choose to humbly accept it from God. When we truly humble ourselves under His mighty hand, we'll in due time experience the sufficiency of His grace, for "God opposes the proud, but gives grace to the humble" (James 4:6).

Such humility leads easily to worship. Looking upward, we see God in all His majesty, power, glory, and sovereignty as well as His mercy, goodness, and grace. Looking at ourselves, we recognize our dependence upon God and our sinfulness before Him. We see our sovereign Creator as worthy to be worshiped, served, and obeyed and ourselves as mere creatures, unworthy sinners who so often fail to worship and obey Him.

We deserve nothing from God but eternal judgment. We're continuous debtors, not only for His sovereign mercy in saving us but for every breath we draw, every bite of food we eat. We have no rights before God. Everything is of His grace. Everything in our lives belongs to Him, and He tells us (in the landowner's words to his vineyard workers), "Am I not allowed to do what I choose with what belongs to me?" (Matthew 20:15).

Here is another dimension of God's sovereignty: His absolute right to do with us as He pleases. That He has chosen to redeem us and send His Son to die for us, instead of sending us to hell, is due solely to His sovereign mercy and grace.

Heartfelt worship and thanksgiving in our adversity is a frank acknowledgment that whatever we have at any given moment—health, position, wealth, or whatever we may cherish—is always a gift from God's sovereign grace and may be taken away at His pleasure. Yet God acts toward us in love, mercy, and grace, all the while working to conform us to the likeness of Christ.

As we bow in worship before His almighty power, we can also bow in confidence that He exercises that power for us, not against us. Therefore, we should bow in an attitude of humility, accepting His dealings in our lives. And we can also bow in love, knowing that those dealings, however severe and painful they may seem, come from a wise and caring heavenly Father.

THE TRUST THAT BRINGS GLORY TO GOD

Our heart is glad in him, because
we trust in his holy name.
PSALM 33:21

As we grow in trusting God, our highest response to adversity should be to seek His glory.

We see this attitude illustrated in the life of the apostle Paul during his imprisonment in Rome. Not only was he imprisoned but he knew of supposedly fellow ministers of the gospel who were actually trying to add to his troubles by their preaching (see Philippians 1:14-17). What was Paul's response?

He said, "But what does it matter? The important thing is that in every way, whether from false motives or true, Christ is preached. And because of this I rejoice" (verse 18, NIV). It really didn't matter to Paul how he was affected by adversities; the important thing to him was what happened to the gospel.

Most of us probably haven't progressed that far in our Christian maturity. We haven't attained to the degree of self-lessness that Paul evidenced. To us, it still matters what happens to us. But Paul's example should be our goal, and if we watch for opportunities to grow in that direction, we'll see them.

Perhaps you have a certain position of responsibility in your church. Suppose someone comes along who's more gifted than you and you're asked (perhaps not very graciously) to step aside in favor of that person. How will you respond? Here's your opportunity to grow in the direction of being concerned for only God's glory. If you'll respond to God in this and humble yourself under His mighty hand, you'll experience His grace enabling you to be concerned primarily—if not entirely—with His glory. You'll have grown more into the likeness of Jesus, who laid aside His glory to die for you.

Above all, you must see the hand of God in this event, knowing that He who does all things well intends this only for your good.

A quotation from the pen of Alexander Carson will help us to not only see this typical event in its proper perspective but also draw together several gracious truths about trusting God:

> Nothing can be more consoling to the man of God than the conviction that the Lord who made the world governs the world; and that every event, great and small, prosperous and adverse, is under the absolute disposal of him who doth all things well, and who regulates all things for the good of his people. . . . The Christian will be confident and courageous in duty, in proportion as he views God in His Providence as ruling in the midst of his enemies; and acting for the good of his people, as well as for his own glory, even in the persecution of the Gospel.[20]

So can we trust God?

We have seen that He is indeed trustworthy. He is absolutely sovereign over every event in the universe, and He exercises that sovereignty in an infinitely wise and loving way for our good. We have every reason to trust God, for He will never fail us nor forsake us.

But can *you* trust God? Is your total relationship with Him one on which you can build a bulwark of trust against the attacks of adversity? You cannot trust God in isolation from all other areas of your life. To grow in your ability to trust Him in times of adversity, you must first lay a solid foundation of a daily personal relationship with Him. Only as you know Him intimately and seek to obey Him completely will you be able to establish a trust relationship with Him.

And then, to that foundation of a life lived in communion with God, we must add what we learn about Him in Scripture—about His sovereignty, wisdom, and love. We must lay hold of these great truths in the little trials as well as the major calamities of life. As we do this, in dependence upon the enabling power of His Holy Spirit, we'll be able more and more to say,

"I can trust God."

DAY

X

NOTES

1. A. H. Strong, in Dallas Willard, *In Search of Guidance: Developing a Conversational Relationship with God* (Ventura, CA: Regal, 1984), 91.

2. Margaret Clarkson, *Grace Grows Best in Winter* (Grand Rapids, MI: Eerdmans, 1984), 40–41.

3. Charles Bridges, *An Exposition of the Book of Proverbs* (Evansville, IN: Sovereign Grace Book Club, 1959), 364.

4. Lina Sandell Berg, "Day By Day," trans. Andrew L. Skoog, 1865.

5. Ken Barker, *NIV Study Bible* (Grand Rapids, MI: Zondervan, 1985), at Psalm 139:13.

6. James Hufstetler, "On Knowing Oneself," *The Banner of Truth*, Issue 280 (January 1987), 13.

7. J. Dewey, comp., *Selections from the Writings of George MacDonald: Helps for Weary Souls* (Chicago: Purdy Publishing, 1889), 34–35.

8. Hufstetler, 14.

9. J. R. Miller, *Finding One's Mission* (Swengel, PA: Reiner Publications, n.d.), 2.

10. J. I. Packer, *Your Father Loves You: Daily Insights for Knowing God* (Wheaton, IL: Harold Shaw Publishers, 1986), devotional reading for October 13.

11. Fanny J. Crosby, "All the Way My Savior Leads Me," *Brightest and Best* (New York: Biglow & Main, 1875).

12. Horatius Bonar, *When God's Children Suffer* (New Canaan, CT: Keats Publishing, 1981; originally published as *Night of Weeping*), 31.

13. Bonar, 28–29.

14. Daniel Dyke, quoted in C. H. Spurgeon, *The Treasury of David* (Grand Rapids, MI: Baker, 1984), 4:306.

15. Clarkson, 21.

16. These renderings of Hebrews 13:5 are from *The New Testament in Modern Speech* (Weymouth), ©1903, 1904, 1909, 1912, trans. Richard Francis Weymouth, ed. and rev. Ernest Hampden-Cook; *Young's Literal Translation of the Bible* by Robert Young (1899); and the *Amplified New Testament* ©1958, 1987 by The Lockman Foundation.

17. John Newton, *The Works of John Newton* (Edinburgh: Banner of Truth, 1985), 5:624.

18. John Brown, *Expository Discourses on 1 Peter* (Edinburgh: Banner of Truth, 1975), 2:539.

19. Philip Bennett Power, *The "I Wills" of the Psalms* (Edinburgh: Banner of Truth, 1985), 10, 8.

20. Alexander Carson, *History of Providence As Manifested in Scripture: Or Facts from Scripture Illustrative of the Government of God* (New York: Edward H. Fletcher, 1854), 168–169.

ABOUT THE AUTHOR

JERRY BRIDGES is a well-respected author and conference speaker. His most popular book, *The Pursuit of Holiness*, has sold more than one million copies. Jerry has been on staff with The Navigators for over fifty years and currently serves in the Collegiate Mission, where he is involved primarily in staff development.

SUPPORT THE MINISTRY OF THE NAVIGATORS

The Navigators' calling is to advance the gospel of Jesus and His kingdom into the nations through spiritual generations of laborers living and discipling among the lost.

Navigators have invested their lives in people for more than 75 years, coming alongside them life on life to help them passionately know Christ and to make Him known.

The U.S. Navigators' ministry touches lives in varied settings, including college campuses, military bases, downtown offices, urban neighborhoods, prisons, and youth camps.

Dedicated to helping people navigate spiritually, The Navigators aims to make a permanent difference in the lives of people around the world. The Navigators helps its communities of friends to follow Christ passionately and equip them effectively to go out and do the same.

To learn more about donating to The Navigators' ministry, go to **www.navigators.org/us/support** or call toll-free at **1-866-568-7827**.

THE NAVIGATORS®